asian
perfection

HINKLER
BOOKS

asian
perfection

Food Editor
Ellen Argyriou

Creative Director
Sam Grimmer

Project Editor
Lara Morcombe

HINKLER BOOKS

First published in 2004 by Hinkler Books Pty Ltd
17–23 Redwood Drive
Dingley, VIC 3172 Australia
www.hinklerbooks.com

First printed in 2004

© Text and Design Hinkler Books Pty Ltd
© Step-by-Step Shots and Hero Shots on page 47 Hinkler Books Pty Ltd
© Hero Shots on pages 12, 13, 14, 15, 16, 17, 18, 19, 20, 21, 24, 25, 26, 27, 28,
29, 30, 31, 34-35, 36-37, 39, 40, 41, 42-43, 46, 48-49, 50, 51, 52-53, 54, 55,
56, 57, 60, 61, 62-63, 64-65, 66, 67, 69, 69, 70-71, 72, 73
R&R Publications licensed to Hinkler Books Pty Ltd

ISBN: 1 74121 827 6
EAN: 9 781741 218275

Printed and bound in China

contents

an introduction to asian cooking

The largest continent on earth, Asia is home to an exciting and diverse range of cuisines. In Western countries Chinese, Japanese, Indian, Thai and Vietnamese food outlets have been a welcome addition to the restaurant scene. The popularity of Asian food has grown immeasurably and with it a desire to make this cuisine part of home-cooked family meals. Supermarkets now stock a considerable range of the necessary Asian ingredients, both grocery lines and fresh Asian vegetables, herbs and flavourings. This book will help you to prepare a healthy Asian meal, packed full of flavour.

stocking the pantry

The following guide will assist you to select a basic supply.

sauces

Listed are the most widely used Asian sauces – it is essential to stock 2–3 of these in your pantry.

soy sauce: A thin brown sauce made from soy beans, wheat, yeast and salt. It is aged and distilled to make the sauce. It is widely used in Asian cooking. Light soy sauce is light in colour and density and will flavour foods without adding colour. Dark soy sauce is darker, thicker and richer in flavour as it is aged longer than the light soy. It gives a rich brown colour to the food. Indonesian soy or kecap manis is thick, dark and sweet. For a similar result use dark soy sauce and add brown sugar. All soy sauces will keep indefinitely on the pantry shelf.

oyster sauce: This sauce is made by fermenting dried oysters with soy sauce and brine. It adds a rich savoury flavour to meat and vegetable dishes and is also used in stir-fries. Be sure to store it in the refrigerator after opening.

hoisin sauce: Hoisin is made from fermented soya beans, garlic, chilli and spices. Sweet and spicy in flavour it is used as a condiment or to add to pork, chicken or beef dishes. It can be interchanged with oyster sauce in recipes, and can be stored on a pantry shelf.

chilli sauce: Various varieties are available. Choose one to suit your tastes. Chinese sweet chilli sauce is a hot sweet and sour sauce. It is added in small quantities to fish dishes and stir-fries. Thai chilli sauce or náam phrík is used mainly as a table condiment. Some are hot and strong, flavoured with shrimp paste and fish sauce. Milder varieties are available and are used as a dipping sauce. Store these sauces in the refrigerator after opening.

fish sauce: An important ingredient in Southeast Asian cuisine. A little added to the cooking has a major impact on flavour. It is made from fermented whitebait and salt. Fish sauce adds a pungent flavour to dipping sauces,

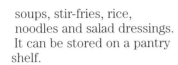

soups, stir-fries, rice, noodles and salad dressings. It can be stored on a pantry shelf.

black bean sauce: Made from fermented black soya beans, chilli and spices. Used in stir-fry meat, or mixed stir-fries. Hot bean or sweet bean sauce is available. It should be stored in the refrigerator after opening.

shrimp sauce: Much like fish sauce but made with small shrimps or prawns and brine. It resembles anchovy paste, which is often used as a substitute. It can be stored on the pantry shelf.

spices, curry and other flavouring agents

five-spice powder: A very popular spice in Chinese cookery. It is a ground mixture of anise, pepper, star anise, cloves, cinnamon and fennel.

turmeric: A plant root that has been dried and powdered. It gives a mild flavour but is prized for the colour it gives to food, particularly rice. It is included in curry powder mixes for that purpose.

cumin: An essential ingredient in prepared curry powder mixes. It has a delightful fragrance and goes well with beef and lamb.

dried coriander seed or ground coriander: The dried seeds of the fresh coriander plant. It gives a delightful fragrance to food.

tamarind liquid: Tamarind liquid is an important flavouring agent in Indian, Indonesian and Malayan cooking. The long fibres of the tamarind pod are soaked in water to extract the flavour, the pulp is discarded and the liquid is used. Dried tamarind pulp is sold in packets. There is also a bottled tamarind liquid available, perhaps not as good as soaking the pulp to make the liquid.

curry: Curry is the word that refers to the sauce around braised meat and chicken. The

spice mixes used to make curry in India and Southeast Asia are individually blended according to the fragrance and strength of heat desired. For convenience curry powder (a ready mix blend of spices for the sauce) became commercially available a long time ago. The blends now cater to a wider range of tastes. Curry pastes, which are spice blends roasted in oil, represent particular spice blends, eg, Thai red or green curry paste and rendang curry paste. In your pantry, stock a mild and fragrant curry powder or paste. If a hotter taste is required, add a little chilli powder. Store dry powders on the pantry shelf and curry pastes in the refrigerator after opening

dried shrimps: A little dried shrimp is used to give a delightful flavour to food. Soak as directed and store in a tightly closed jar on a pantry shelf.

white miso: Important in Japanese cuisine, it's used to flavour stocks and soups. It is made from yellow soya beans, boiled and crushed, then allowed to ferment. It should be stored in the refrigerator.

rice wine: A wine made from rice. Mirin, a sweet rice wine, is also used.

dry and sweet sherry: If you are fond of Chinese cooking, a bottle of either is useful in your pantry.

rice vinegar: Rice vinegar is clear to pale gold in colour, with a mildly sweet flavour. It's used in dipping sauces and salad dressings. A little sweet sherry may be substituted.

palm sugar: Palm sugar is obtained from the sap of the coconut and palmyra palm trees. It has a strong sweet flavour. Dark brown sugar is a good substitute.

rice and dried noodles

Rice and dried noodles are the staples of Asian cuisine and you should always have a cache readily available in your pantry.

short-grain or medium-grain rice: These varieties are used mainly with Chinese cooking.

jasmine and basmati: Both are a long-grain rice and are preferred with Indian and Malaysian dishes.

glutinous rice: Also known as sticky rice, this rice is used mainly in sweet dishes. It clings together when cooked and blends well with sugar and coconut milk.

dried rice noodles: Also known as rice sticks or rice vermicelli, soak dried rice noodles in hot water until soft, drain well and use in stir-fries or soups. When deep-fried in their dried state they puff up to a crunchy texture to use in salads or to top a stir-fry.

bean thread noodles: Made from mung bean starch, bean thread noodles are also known

as cellophane noodles. Soak in hot water before use, drain and use in stir-fries, soups or salads.

wheat noodles: Available in various widths and either plain or enriched with egg, wheat noodles need to be boiled and drained well before inclusion in a dish.

Supermarkets stock a large range of instant noodles or quick cooking noodles. Some include a flavour sachet. They can be added to a quick stir-fry after cooking as directed on the pack.

fresh asian ingredients

Fresh flavouring ingredients are important in Asian cooking.

garlic: For a mild flavour, fry slices of garlic in the oil then remove before the addition of other ingredients. A more defined flavour is achieved if garlic is finely chopped and included with the other ingredients. Use fresh garlic. Garlic cloves are best stored in a jar in the refrigerator.

ginger: Ginger is an essential flavouring ingredient. Cut a 1–2 cm piece from the ginger root. Peel thinly and slice very finely or grate. Any remaining ginger root may be wrapped in damp paper, placed in a plastic bag and stored in the refrigerator crisper for 2–3 weeks.

lemon grass: This imparts a characteristic sour flavour to Asian dishes. Trim away the outer blades and cut the white bulbous part into thin slices or chop finely. Lemon grass will keep in the refrigerator crisper for up to 2 months.

chillies: Small, red, hot chillies must be handled with care. If an intense hot flavour is needed, chop the chilli with the seeds and vein. If a milder heat is desired, split the chilli and remove the seeds and thick vein. The hot part of the chilli is concentrated in the seeds and vein, and will remain on your fingers. If, after handling chillies, you touch your tongue, lips or eyes, severe irritation will result. Wash your hands immediately after handling chillies or wear rubber gloves.

coconut milk and cream: Is made from fresh, grated coconut 'meat'. Canned coconut milk is available as either thin or thick. Thin coconut milk is used for long simmering with other ingredients. Thick coconut milk or cream is added at the end of the recipe to give flavour and a smooth consistency. Store left over coconut milk or cream in a sealed container in the refrigerator for up to 1 week. It may also be frozen for longer storage, but loses some of its smooth texture.

fresh noodles: A wide variety may be found in the refrigerator cabinets at supermarkets as well as in Asian food stores. Varieties include Hokkien noodles and the thinner Singapore noodles, both made from wheat flour. Rice noodles include the Japanese udon and the flat pad thai, which are gluten free.

meat: Many Asian recipes call for thinly sliced meat, particularly for a stir-fry. Always cut the meat across the grain for a tender result. Purchase the meat in a thick piece or 'nut' not a slice, to be able to cut across the grain. For thinly sliced meat, freeze the meat for 2 hours to keep it firm under the blade of the knife. Trays of stir-fry strips or small cubed meats are available in butcher shops and supermarkets.

wrappers: These are squares of noodle dough used to wrap food in to make spring rolls and wontons. Both rice and wheat-based wrappers are available. They can be found in the refrigerator cabinets at supermarkets and Asian food stores.

soups
salads
and
starters

thai fish sticks with cucumber salad

ingredients

salad

1 cucumber, peeled and thinly sliced
4 tablespoons white-wine vinegar
4 tablespoons white sugar
1 large red or green chilli, deseeded and finely chopped
1 small spring onion (green onion), thinly sliced

fish sticks

small handful fresh coriander
4 spring onions, chopped
450 g (14 oz) cod or other skinless white fish fillet, cubed
3 tablespoons red curry paste
1 teaspoon salt
2 teaspoons lime juice
1 large egg white
12 stalks lemon grass

serves 4

i

preparation time
25 minutes

cooking time
6 minutes

nutritional value per serve
fat: 2.6 g
carbohydrate: 8.3 g
protein: 9.4 g

1 Combine cucumber, vinegar, sugar, chilli and 1 small spring onion with 4 tablespoons of cold water. Cover and set aside in a cool place.

2 Place coriander and remaining spring onions in a food processor and process until finely chopped. Add fish, curry paste, salt and lime juice and process until the fish is finely chopped. Add egg white and continue processing until the mixture is stiff.

3 Divide the fish mixture into 12 portions, then carefully press each around a lemon grass stick, forming a 'sausage' shape. Preheat the grill to high. Place the fish sticks on a lightly oiled baking sheet and grill for 6 minutes, turning once, until cooked and lightly browned on all sides. Serve with the cucumber salad.

japanese prawn and vegetable tempura

ingredients

1 zucchini (courgette)
salt
4 green prawns
1 red capsicum (pepper)
1 large egg
150 g (5 oz) plain flour
$^1/_2$ cup (125 ml, 4 fl oz) ice-cold water
peanut oil for deep-frying
lime wedges to serve
soy sauce to serve
serves 4

preparation time
25 minutes, plus
20 minutes
standing

cooking time
10 minutes

**nutritional value
per serve**
fat: 1.4 g
carbohydrate: 19 g
protein: 7.2 g

1 Cut the zucchini in half across the centre, trim the end and cut each half lengthways into 4. Sprinkle with salt and set aside for 20 minutes. Shell the prawns, leaving tails attached. Devein, using a sharp knife. Rinse and refrigerate. Deseed the capsicum and cut into 8 strips.

2 Break the egg into a mixing bowl. Mix in the ice-cold water and fold in the flour to make a lumpy batter.

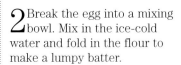

3 Heat 5 cm of oil in a wok or frying pan. Coat the zucchini slices in batter and deep-fry for 3 minutes or until

golden, turning halfway through. Drain on kitchen towels and keep warm. Repeat with capsicum strips. Coat prawns and cook for 1 minute. Serve immediately with lime wedges and soy sauce.

1 Into a large bowl, place chickpea flour, ground rice, bicarbonate of soda, chilli powder, turmeric, curry powder and salt. Gradually add water, stirring constantly until smooth. Add spring onions, zucchini and eggplant and combine well.

2 Pour the oil into a wok to a depth of 5 cm and heat over a medium to high heat. Check oil is hot enough by dropping in a small piece of vegetable – it should sizzle. Gently drop heaped tablespoons of mixture, 4 at a time, into the hot oil and fry for 2–3 minutes until golden. Turn over and cook for a further 2–3 minutes until crisp. Remove with a slotted spoon and drain on kitchen towels. Serve with mint and cucumber raita. Recipe opposite.

vegetable bhajis

ingredients

10 spring onions (green onions), finely chopped
2 zucchinis (courgettes), coarsely grated
1 eggplant (aubergine), finely diced
vegetable oil for frying
batter
100 g (3¹/₂ oz) chickpea flour
50 g (2 oz) ground rice
¹/₄ teaspoon bicarbonate of soda
1 teaspoon chilli powder
1 teaspoon turmeric
1-2 tablespoons mild or hot curry powder
1 teaspoon salt
225 ml (7¹/₂ fl oz) water
serves 4

preparation time
25 minutes

cooking time
30 minutes

nutritional value
per serve
fat: 0.5 g
carbohydrate: 13 g
protein: 2.5 g

cucumber and mint raita

hour. Drain through a strainer, pressing out as much liquid as possible. Dry in 2 layers of absorbent paper.

2 In a clean bowl, place cucumbers and toss in mint.

3 In another bowl, combine garlic, ginger, yoghurt and lemon juice. Add to the cucumbers and toss well to combine. Refrigerate for 1 hour. Serve with the vegetable bhajis or to accompany a curry dish.

preparation time
10 minutes, plus
1 hour standing
and 1 hour
refrigeration

**nutritional value
per serve**
fat: 1.8 g
carbohydrate: 4 g
protein: 2.6 g

ingredients

2 large cucumbers
2 teaspoons salt
2 tablespoons fresh mint leaves, chopped
1 small clove garlic, crushed
$1/4$ teaspoon finely grated fresh ginger
1 cup (250 ml, 8 fl oz) natural yoghurt
2 teaspoons lemon juice
serves 4

1 Peel cucumbers and slice very thinly. Place in a bowl and sprinkle with salt, toss to mix salt through. Stand for 1

spring rolls

ingredients

20 g (²/₃ oz) vermicelli
3 tablespoons vegetable oil
3 cloves garlic, finely chopped
310 g (10 oz) minced chicken
¹/₄ cabbage, cut into fine strips
1 carrot, cut into thin strips
2 spring onions (green onions),
  finely chopped
¹/₂ teaspoon salt
1 teaspoon sugar
¹/₂ teaspoon white pepper
1 tablespoon oyster sauce
20-25 rice paper wrappers
1 egg, beaten
extra oil for deep frying
lettuce and mint leaves to serve
makes 20

1 Soak vermicelli in hot water for 5 minutes until soft. Drain, cut into 5 cm lengths and set aside.

preparation time
15 minutes

cooking time
15 minutes

nutritional value per serve
fat: 9.2 g
carbohydrate: 5 g
protein: 9.8 g

2 Heat 3 tablespoons oil in a wok or frying pan, add garlic and chicken and cook for 8 minutes, stirring constantly until crumbly. Add cabbage, carrot, spring onions and vermicelli. Cook on high for about 3 minutes until vegetables soften.

3 Turn off heat. Add salt, sugar, pepper and oyster sauce, stir to mix well and allow to cool. Brush each side of the rice wrappers with water. Place 1 tablespoon of mixture onto each wrapper, turn sides in first, roll and seal each with beaten egg. Refrigerate until needed.

4 Heat extra oil in wok or frying pan. Deep-fry a few rolls at a time until golden. Drain on absorbent paper. Serve on lettuce leaves garnished with mint. Serve with your favourite sweet chilli or plum sauce.

steamed stuffed cucumbers

ingredients

500 g (1 lb) cucumbers
375g (12 oz) can water chestnuts,
    drained and finely chopped
2$^1/_2$ tablespoons glutinous rice flour
sesame oil
$^1/_2$ teaspoon salt
$^1/_2$ teaspoon sugar
1 small carrot, peeled and finely diced
4 black dried mushrooms, soaked,
    drained and finely chopped
$^3/_4$ cup (185 ml, 6 fl oz) water
1$^1/_2$ teaspoons cornflour
serves 4-6

1 Thinly peel cucumbers and cut into 1 cm thick slices. Scoop out seeds with a teaspoon leaving a base layer. Place cucumber shells in boiling water for 1 minute. Rinse in cold water, drain and dust inside with a little cornflour.

2 In a bowl, place finely diced water chestnuts, glutinous rice flour, sesame oil and half the salt and sugar. Add carrot and mushrooms and mix well. Pile high into the cucumber circles. Place circles on a plate and set on steaming rack over hot water in a wok. Cover and steam for 15–20 minutes.

3 Place a drop of sesame oil, the remaining salt and sugar and the water into a small saucepan and bring to the boil. Blend the cornflour with a little water, add to the saucepan and stir until liquid boils and thickens. Cool to warm. Spoon over each steamed cucumber ring to glaze. Allow to cool. Serve at room temperature.

i

preparation time
15 minutes

cooking time
15 minutes

**nutritional value
per serve**
fat: 1.7 g
carbohydrate: 7 g
protein: 0.8 g

balinese chicken satay

ingredients

1 stalk lemon grass
1 onion, chopped
1 clove garlic, chopped
2 teaspoons ground coriander
1 teaspoon turmeric
juice of $1/2$ lemon
1 teaspoon salt
3 chicken breast fillets, cut into 1 cm cubes
$1/2$ cucumber, pared into ribbons with a
    vegetable peeler, to serve

satay sauce

1 small onion, chopped
1 clove garlic, chopped
1 tablespoon peanut oil
1 teaspoon chilli powder
155 ml (5 fl oz) can coconut milk
75 g ($2^1/_2$ oz) roasted salted peanuts,
    finely ground
1 tablespoon soft dark brown sugar
1 tablespoon fresh lemon juice

serves 4

1 Peel the outer layer from the lemon grass and chop the lower white bulbous part, discarding the fibrous top. Process to a paste with the onion, garlic, coriander, turmeric, lemon juice and 1 teaspoon of salt in a food processor.

i

preparation time
30 minutes, plus 2
hours marinating

cooking time
25 minutes

**nutritional value
per serve**
fat: 12.9 g
carbohydrate: 4 g
protein: 8.9 g

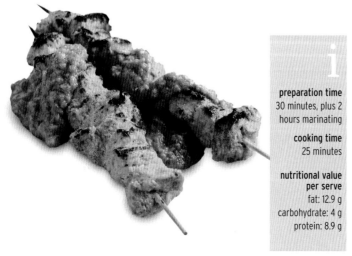

2 Place the chicken in a non-metallic bowl and coat with the paste. Cover and marinate in the refrigerator for 2 hours, or overnight. If using wooden skewers, soak them in water for 10 minutes.

3 To make the satay sauce, process the onion and garlic to a paste in a food processor. Heat the oil in a heavy-based saucepan and fry the paste for 5 minutes, stirring. Mix in the chilli powder, then the remaining sauce ingredients. Bring to the boil, stirring, then simmer for 10 minutes.

4 Preheat the grill to high. Thread the chicken onto 8 skewers. Grill for 10 minutes, turning once, until cooked. Serve with the cucumber ribbons and satay sauce.

vietnamese herb salad rolls with peanut sauce

ingredients

55 g (2 oz) cellophane noodles
3 tablespoons rice vinegar
1 tablespoon fish sauce
4 tablespoons roasted peanuts, crushed
12 large cooked prawns, finely chopped
20 thai basil leaves, finely sliced
10 asian mint leaves, finely sliced
a handful fresh coriander, finely chopped
4 leaves bok choy (pak choi), finely shredded
2 cabbage leaves, very finely shredded
5 spring onions (green onions), finely sliced lengthwise
1 medium carrot, grated
1 packet 20 cm square rice paper wrappers

sauce

2 tablespoons peanut oil
5 cloves garlic, crushed
$^{1}/_{2}$ small red chilli, minced
5 tablespoons peanut butter
$1^{1}/_{2}$ tablespoons tomato paste
3 tablespoons hoi sin sauce
1 teaspoon sugar
1 teaspoon fish sauce
$^{3}/_{4}$ cup (185 ml, 6 fl oz) water
40 g ($1^{1}/_{4}$ oz) peanuts, crushed

makes 16–20

1 In a bowl of hot water, soak the cellophane noodles for 5–10 minutes until tender, drain immediately and rinse with cold water. Cut noodles with scissors to a manageable length. In a large bowl, toss noodles with vinegar, fish sauce, roasted peanuts and prawns. Add the prepared fresh herbs, bok choy, cabbage, spring onions and carrot. Toss well.

2 Working with 1 wrapper at a time, soak the rice wrapper in warm water for 30 seconds and lie on a flat surface. Place a heaped tablespoon of filling on the wrapper about 2 cm in from front edge and sides. Fold front edge over the filling, fold in the side edges and roll up. Repeat with the remaining ingredients.

3 Heat the oil in a saucepan and sauté the garlic and minced chilli for about 2 minutes until softened. Add all remaining sauce ingredients and whisk while heating. Bring to the boil and simmer about 3 minutes until thickened slightly. To serve, slice each roll on the diagonal, then rest one half over the other. Serve the sauce separately in a small pot for dipping.

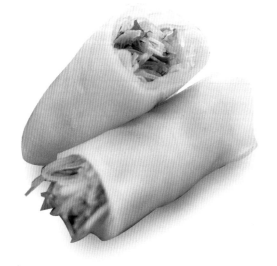

i

preparation time
20 minutes

cooking time
10 minutes

nutritional value per serve
fat: 9.8 g
carbohydrate: 7.1 g
protein: 13.6 g

leek, lime and coconut soup

ingredients

2 tablespoons olive oil
3 leeks, thinly sliced
1 green chilli, deseeded and chopped
2 potatoes, diced
grated rind (zest) and juice of 2 limes
salt and black pepper
600 ml (1 pint) vegetable stock
225 ml (7¹/₂ fl oz) can coconut milk
fresh coriander to garnish
extra lime slices to garnish
serves 4

1 In a large heavy-based saucepan, heat the oil and add the leeks, chilli, potatoes, lime rind and seasoning. Cook for 2 minutes, add stock and bring to the boil. Reduce the heat and simmer for 20–25 minutes, until the potatoes are tender. Leave to cool slightly.

2 In a food processor, blend soup briefly to make a chunky, creamy mixture. Return soup to the pan.

3 Stir in the lime juice, then add the coconut milk and heat through, taking care not to let the soup boil. Serve hot or cold, garnished with coriander and slices of lime.

i

preparation time
15 minutes

cooking time
30 minutes

nutritional value per serve
fat: 5.1 g
carbohydrate: 4 g
protein: 1.5 g

curried cream of vegetable soup

ingredients

3 tablespoons peanut oil
2 tablespoons curry powder
pinch of ground cinnamon
pinch of nutmeg
pinch of turmeric
pinch of ginger
3 carrots, diced
2 onions, chopped
2 cloves garlic, chopped
2 potatoes, diced
2 zucchini (courgettes), diced
1 litre (1²/₃ pints) vegetable stock
300 g (10 oz) can cannellini beans, drained
220 g (7¹/₂ oz) can red kidney beans, drained
185 ml (6 fl oz) crème fraîche
salt
2 teaspoons flat-leaf parsley, chopped for garnish

serves 4

i

preparation time
20 minutes

cooking time
30 minutes

nutritional value
per serve
fat: 4.3 g
carbohydrate: 5.7 g
protein: 2.8 g

1 In a large heavy-based saucepan, place the oil and add the curry powder, cinnamon, nutmeg, turmeric and ginger. Cook for 1 minute, then add carrots, onions, garlic, potatoes and zucchini. Stir to coat thoroughly in the oil and spice mixture, and cook for a further 5 minutes. Add the stock and bring to the boil. Reduce the heat and simmer for 20 minutes or until the vegetables are tender.

2 Add the cannellini and red kidney beans and gently heat through. Remove from the heat and stir in the crème fraîche. Season to taste and serve sprinkled with the parsley.

thai hot and sour prawn soup

ingredients

2 stalks lemon grass
300 g (10 oz) green prawns, with head
  and shell on
1 tablespoon vegetable oil
1 litre (1²/₃ pints) chicken stock
1 clove garlic, crushed
2.5 cm piece fresh root ginger,
  roughly chopped
grated rind (zest) of 1 lime and juice
  of 2 limes
1 green chilli, deseeded and finely
  chopped
salt and black pepper
1 tablespoon thai fish sauce
1 red chilli, deseeded and sliced
2 tablespoons fresh chopped coriander
  to garnish
serves 4

1 Peel the outer layers from the lemon grass stalks and chop the lower white bulbous parts into 3 pieces, discarding the fibrous tops. Shell the prawns, leaving the tails attached and reserving the shells for the stock. Cut a slit along the back of each prawn with a sharp knife and remove the thin black vein. Rinse the prawns, then refrigerate until needed.

2 In a large saucepan, heat the oil and fry the prawn shells for 2–3 minutes, until pink. Add the stock, garlic, ginger, lemon grass, lime rind, green chilli and salt to taste. Bring to the boil, then reduce the heat, cover and simmer for 20 minutes.

3 Strain the stock and return to the pan. Stir in fish sauce and lime juice and bring to the boil. Add the prawns, reduce the heat and simmer for 3 minutes or until the prawns turn pink and are cooked through. Season with pepper and serve garnished with red chilli and coriander.

i

preparation time
25 minutes

cooking time
30 minutes

**nutritional value
per serve**
fat: 1.6 g
carbohydrate: 0.6 g
protein: 5.1 g

vegetable saffron samosas

ingredients

vegetable saffron filling

1 tablespoon peanut oil
1 teaspoon sesame oil
1 onion, finely chopped
1 tablespoon finely grated fresh ginger
1 teaspoon ground cumin
1 potato, peeled and finely chopped
1 carrot, finely chopped
¼ teaspoon saffron threads, soaked in
 1 tablespoon hot water
1 red capsicum (pepper), finely chopped
60 g (2 oz) frozen peas

pastry

315 g (10 oz) flour
1 tablespoon baking powder
1 tablespoon castor sugar
4 tablespoons lard
1 cup (250 ml, 8 fl oz) warm water

sun-dried capsicum dipping sauce

125 g (4 oz) sun-dried capsicums,
 chopped
1 cup (250 ml, 8 fl oz) mayonnaise
1 tablespoon white-wine vinegar

makes 20

preparation time
20 minutes

cooking time
28 minutes

**nutritional value
per serve**
fat: 10.6 g
carbohydrate: 25 g
protein: 4.1 g

1 To make filling, heat peanut and sesame oils together in a wok over medium heat, add onion, ginger and cumin and stir-fry for 3 minutes or until onion is golden. In a bowl, combine potato, carrot and saffron. Add to wok and stir-fry for 10 minutes until potato is tender Add red capsicum and peas and stir-fry for another 5 minutes. Remove mixture from wok and set aside to cool.

2 To make pastry, place flour, baking powder, sugar and lard in a food processor and process until mixture resembles fine breadcrumbs. With machine running, gradually add water and process until mixture forms a soft dough. Turn dough onto a lightly floured surface and knead until smooth and glossy. Cover and rest for 10 minutes.

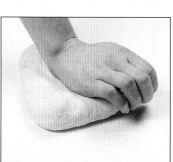

3 Divide dough into 20 equal pieces and shape into balls. Roll out each dough ball to form a 10 cm circle. Place a tablespoon of filling on one half leaving a 1½ cm border. Brush edges lightly with water, fold pastry over filling and press edges together to seal.

4 Half fill a clean wok with hot water and bring to the boil. Place samosas in a bamboo steamer lined with nonstick baking paper. Pierce holes in the paper to allow steam through. Cover steamer, place on a wire rack in wok and steam for 10 minutes or until pastry is cooked.

5 To make sauce, place sun-dried capsicums, mayonnaise and vinegar in a food processor or blender and process until smooth.

hot and sour fish soup

ingredients

1 kg (2 lb) firm fleshed fish (red snapper)
1½ tablespoons fish sauce
¼ teaspoon white pepper
1 spring onion (green onion), chopped
1.5 litres (2½ pints) water
2 stalks lemongrass, cut into 5 cm
    lengths and crushed lightly
55 g (2 oz) tamarind pulp
¾ cup (185 ml, 6 fl oz) boiling water
1 tablespoon sugar
185 g (6 oz) bamboo shoots, sliced
160 g (5½ oz) pineapple, sliced
2 tomatoes, cut into wedges
90 g (3 oz) beansprouts
2 handfuls mixed vietnamese herbs
    (coriander, bitter herb, asian basil)
1 lime, cut into wedges to serve
1 chilli, sliced to serve
serves 4-6

1 Remove head, fins and tail from fish and cut into 8–10 large pieces. In a bowl, combine fish, fish sauce, pepper and spring onion. Set aside to marinate for 15 minutes.

2 Place 6 cups water in a large saucepan and bring to the boil. Add the fish with the marinade and lemongrass. Reduce heat and simmer for 20 minutes. In a bowl, combine tamarind pulp and the ¾ cup boiling water and allow to soak for 15 minutes.

3 Strain the tamarind pulp through a fine strainer, discarding the pulp. Add to the saucepan along with the sugar, bamboo shoots, pineapple and tomatoes. Simmer for 4–5 minutes until fish is tender.

4 Divide bean sprouts between serving bowls and spoon over hot soup. Sprinkle over mixed vietnamese herbs. Serve with lime wedges and sliced chilli on the side.

i

preparation time
30 minutes,
plus 15 minutes
marinating
cooking time
15 minutes

**nutritional value
per serve**
fat: 0.7 g
carbohydrate: 2 g
protein: 6.1 g

warm thai lamb salad

ingredients

250 g (8 oz) assorted lettuce leaves, washed and crisped
1 cucumber, sliced lengthwise into thin ribbons
2 teaspoons vegetable oil
500 g (1 lb) lamb fillets, trimmed and thinly sliced

coriander and chilli dressing

2 tablespoons chopped fresh coriander
1 tablespoon brown sugar
4 tablespoons soy sauce
2 tablespoons sweet chilli sauce
2 tablespoons lime juice
2 teaspoons fish sauce

serves 4

1 In a bowl, combine coriander, sugar, soy and chilli sauces, lime juice and fish sauce. Set aside.

2 Arrange lettuce leaves and cucumber on a serving platter and set aside.

3 Heat oil in a wok over a high heat, add lamb and stir-fry for 2 minutes or until brown. Place lamb on top of lettuce leaves, drizzle with dressing and serve immediately.

i

preparation time
10 minutes

cooking time
2 minutes

nutritional value per serve
fat: 2.7 g
carbohydrate: 2.6 g
protein: 10.6 g

poultry and meat

creamy chicken korma

ingredients

3 tablespoons vegetable oil
1 onion, chopped
2 cloves garlic, crushed
3 tablespoons plain flour
2 tablespoons mild korma curry powder
750 g (1½ lb) chicken breast fillets,
 cut into 2.5 cm cubes
350 ml (11½ fl oz) chicken stock
25 g (1 oz) raisins
1 tablespoon chopped fresh coriander
1 teaspoon garam masala
juice of ½ lemon
4 tablespoons sour cream
fried onion rings for garnish (optional)

serves 4

preparation time
15 minutes

cooking time
30 minutes

**nutritional value
per serve**
fat: 7.8 g
carbohydrate: 4.1 g
protein: 12 g

1 Heat the oil in a large heavy-based saucepan, add the onion and garlic and cook gently for 5 minutes or until softened.

2 Into a bowl, place the flour and curry powder and mix together. Toss the chicken in the seasoned flour, coating well. Reserve the remaining flour. Add the chicken to the onion and garlic, then cook, stirring, for 3–4 minutes until lightly browned. Stir in the seasoned flour and cook for 1 minute.

3 Add the stock and raisins and bring to the boil, stirring. Cover and simmer for 15 minutes. Add the coriander and garam masala and cook for a further 5 minutes. Remove the pan from the heat and stir in the lemon juice and sour cream. Return to a low heat and warm through, taking care not to let the mixture boil.

fragrant duck with pineapple

ingredients

2 (about 175 g, 6 oz each) boneless duck
    breasts, skinned and cut into strips
1 teaspoon five-spice powder
2 tablespoons soy sauce
2 tablespoons rice wine or dry sherry
1 teaspoon sugar
1 tablespoon peanut oil
1 red capsicum (pepper), deseeded and
    cut into thin strips
5 cm piece fresh ginger, cut into
    matchsticks
2 spring onions (green onions), white
    and green parts separated, thinly
    shredded
175 g (6 oz) fresh pineapple, cut into
    bite-sized pieces, plus juice
salt
serves 4

1 Place the duck, five-spice powder, soy sauce, rice wine or sherry and sugar in a shallow non-metallic dish. Cover and marinate for 20 minutes.

2 Remove the duck from the marinade and reserve the marinade. Heat oil in a wok. Stir-fry duck over a high heat for 2 minutes. Add capsicum, ginger and white spring onions and stir-fry for a further 3–4 minutes until capsicum starts to soften.

3 Add pineapple and juice to the wok. Add marinade and stir-fry for 1–2 minutes. Season with salt if necessary. Serve straight away, sprinkled with the spring onions. Serve with plain boiled noodles.

i

preparation time
20 minutes,
plus 20 minutes
marinating

cooking time
10 minutes

**nutritional value
per serve**
fat: 6.2 g
carbohydrate: 4.3 g
protein: 8.6 g

chicken stir-fry with lemon and mango

ingredients

1 ripe mango
2 tablespoons sunflower oil
2 cloves garlic, crushed
2.5 cm piece fresh root ginger, finely chopped
4 chicken breast fillets, cut into strips
150 g (5 oz) snow peas (mangetout), halved lengthways
2 celery sticks, thinly sliced
1 yellow capsicum (pepper), deseeded and cut into matchsticks
4 spring onions (green onions), thinly sliced
sea salt and freshly ground black pepper
juice of 1/2 lemon
2 teaspoons white wine or apple juice
1 tablespoon balsamic vinegar
1 tablespoon clear honey
2 tablespoons chopped fresh coriander

serves 4

i

preparation time
25 minutes

cooking time
10 minutes

nutritional value
fat: 4.4 g
carbohydrate: 3.1 g
protein: 14.1 g

1 Slice the two fatter 'cheeks' of the mango from either side of the stone. Cut a criss-cross pattern across the flesh of each piece to divide into small cubes, then push the skin upwards and slice off the cubes. Set aside.

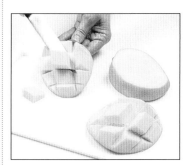

2 Heat the oil in a wok or large frying pan until hot. Add garlic, ginger and chicken and stir fry for 3 minutes. Add snow peas, celery and capsicum and stir-fry for 3–4 minutes. Add the spring onions, mangos and seasoning, and then stir-fry for a further 2 minutes.

3 In a small bowl, combine the lemon juice, white wine or apple juice, balsamic vinegar and honey. Add to the wok and continue to cook for a further 2 minutes. Add the coriander and serve.

beef curry

ingredients

1 kg (2 lb) stewing beef
1 large onion, sliced
4 cloves garlic, crushed
2 tablespoons chopped ginger
2 red chillies, seeded and chopped finely
3$\frac{1}{2}$ tablespoons hot curry powder
2 teaspoons turmeric
1 teaspoon black ground pepper
1$\frac{1}{2}$ teaspoons salt
$\frac{1}{3}$ cup (80 ml, 2$\frac{3}{4}$ fl oz) vegetable oil
1 cup (250 ml, 8 fl oz) water
4$\frac{1}{2}$ tablespoons fish sauce
1 tablespoon sugar
3 large carrots, chopped
3 tablespoons cornflour
2$\frac{1}{4}$ cups (560 ml, 18$\frac{1}{2}$ fl oz) coconut milk
coriander leaves to garnish
serves 4

preparation time
15 minutes,
plus 12 hours
marinating

cooking time
15 minutes

**nutritional value
per serve**
fat: 9.7 g
carbohydrate: 2.7 g
protein: 17.1 g

1 Cut the beef into cubes and place in a non-metallic container. Add onion, garlic, ginger, chillies, curry powder, turmeric, pepper and 1 teaspoon of salt, mix and cover with plastic wrap to dry marinate for 12 hours or overnight. Turn occasionally.

2 In a large, heavy-based saucepan, heat oil on high, add beef, turning to seal all sides. Add the water, $\frac{1}{2}$ teaspoon salt and fish sauce. Bring to the boil, turn heat to low, cover and simmer for 1 hour. Add sugar and carrots and continue cooking for 15–20 minutes until meat is tender.

3 Blend cornflour with a little coconut milk, add to the rest of the coconut milk and pour into the curry. Stir for 10–15 minutes until thickened. Transfer to a serving dish and garnish with coriander leaves.

beef with black bean sauce

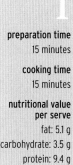

ingredients

450 g (14 oz) sirloin or rump steak, cut into thin strips
1 clove garlic, crushed
1 small red chilli, deseeded and finely chopped (optional)
1 tablespoon dark soy sauce
black pepper
2 teaspoons cornflour
1 tablespoon white-wine vinegar
2 tablespoons vegetable oil
1 red capsicum (pepper), deseeded and cut into strips
1 yellow capsicum, deseeded and cut into strips
1 large zucchini (courgette), cut into matchsticks
150 g (5 oz) snow peas (mangetout), sliced
3 tablespoons black bean stir-fry sauce
4 spring onions (green onions), diagonally sliced
serves 4

i

preparation time
15 minutes

cooking time
15 minutes

nutritional value per serve
fat: 5.1 g
carbohydrate: 3.5 g
protein: 9.4 g

1 In a bowl, combine steak strips, garlic, chilli (if using), soy sauce and seasoning. In another bowl, mix the cornflour with 1 tablespoon of water until smooth, then stir in vinegar.

2 Heat the oil in a wok or large frying pan until very hot. Add the meat and its marinade and stir-fry for 4 minutes, tossing continuously, until seared on all sides.

3 Add capsicum and stir-fry for 2 minutes. Stir in zucchini and snow peas and cook for 3 minutes. Reduce the heat and add the cornflour mixture and black bean sauce. Stir to mix thoroughly and cook for 2 minutes or until the meat and vegetables are cooked through. Scatter with spring onions just before serving. Serve over egg noodles if desired.

roasted tandoori chicken breasts

ingredients

1 teaspoon salt
2 cloves garlic, chopped
2.5 cm piece fresh root ginger, chopped
1 tablespoon chopped fresh coriander
1 tablespoon chopped fresh mint
½ teaspoon turmeric
½ teaspoon hot chilli powder
2 cardamom pods, split, husks
    discarded and seeds reserved
4 tablespoons natural yoghurt
juice of ½ lemon
4 chicken fillets
extra coriander leaves to garnish

serves 4

i

preparation time
15 minutes, plus
6 hours
marinating

cooking time
25 minutes

**nutritional value
per serve**
fat: 5.3 g
carbohydrate: 0.4 g
protein: 19.9 g

1 Grind the salt, garlic, ginger, coriander, mint, turmeric, chilli powder and cardamom seeds to a paste, using a pestle and mortar or coffee grinder. Transfer to a large, non-metallic container, stir in the yoghurt and lemon juice and mix together well.

2 Score each chicken breast 4 times with a sharp knife, then add to the marinade and turn to coat thoroughly. Cover and chill for 6 hours, or overnight.

3 Preheat the oven to 220°C (425°F, gas mark 7). Place the chicken breasts on a rack in a roasting tin and cook for 20–25 minutes, until tender and the juices run clear when pierced with a skewer. Serve with naan bread and salad.

green banana chicken curry

ingredients
salt
1 teaspoon ground turmeric
10 green bananas (plantain), peeled
2 tablespoons vegetable oil
3 spring onions (green onions), chopped
1 tablespoon finely grated fresh ginger
2 small fresh red chillies, seeded and
  chopped
1½ cups (375 ml, 12 fl oz) coconut milk
1 cinnamon stick
45 g (1½ oz) sultanas
30 g (1 oz) roasted cashews
6 chicken breast fillets, cut into thin
  strips
serves 6

1 Combine salt and turmeric and rub over bananas. Heat oil in a wok over a medium heat, add 5 bananas and stir-fry for 5 minutes or until brown. Remove bananas from pan and drain on absorbent kitchen paper. Repeat with remainder adding extra oil if needed.

2 Add spring onions, ginger and chillies to pan and stir-fry for 2 minutes or until mixture is soft. Stir in coconut milk, cinnamon, sultanas, cashews and chicken. Simmer, stirring occasionally, for 20 minutes.

3 Slice bananas, return to pan and simmer, stirring occasionally, for 10 minutes or until chicken is tender. Remove cinnamon stick before serving.

preparation time
10 minutes

cooking time
30 minutes

**nutritional value
per serve**
fat: 6.7 g
carbohydrate: 7 g
protein: 13 g

thai green duck curry with bamboo shoots

ingredients

2 tablespoons vegetable oil
3 tablespoons thai green curry paste
4 boneless duck breasts, skinned and
cut into 2.5 cm cubes
400 ml (13 fl oz) can coconut milk
225 g (7 1/2 oz) can sliced bamboo shoots,
drained
2 tablespoons thai fish sauce
1 teaspoon soft dark brown sugar
salt
2 tablespoons chopped fresh basil
4 tablespoons chopped fresh coriander
extra basil leaves to garnish
serves 4

i

preparation time
10 minutes

cooking time
45 minutes

**nutritional value
per serve**
fat: 18.3 g
carbohydrate: 2 g
protein: 10.4 g

1 Heat the oil in a large, heavy-based saucepan. Add curry paste and fry, stirring frequently, for 3 minutes or until the aromas are released. Add duck, turn to coat thoroughly, and fry for 4–5 minutes, stirring from time to time.

2 Stir in coconut milk, bamboo shoots, fish sauce, sugar and salt to taste. Bring to the boil, stirring often, then reduce the heat. Simmer, uncovered, for 30–35 minutes until the duck is tender, stirring occasionally. Just before serving, stir in the chopped basil and coriander, and garnish with basil leaves.

glazed pork spare ribs

ingredients

1 tablespoon soy sauce

2 tablespoons white-wine vinegar

3 tablespoons hoi sin or oyster sauce

2 tablespoons honey

2 cloves garlic, crushed

2$\frac{1}{2}$ cm piece fresh ginger root, peeled and grated

2 teaspoons vegetable oil

$\frac{1}{2}$ teaspoon five-spice powder

1 tablespoon brown sugar

1.5 -2 kg (3-4 lb) american style pork spareribs

serves 6

1 In a saucepan, combine soy sauce, white-wine vinegar, hoi sin or oyster sauce, honey, garlic, ginger, oil, five-spice powder and sugar. Stir well and bring to the boil. Remove from heat. Place pork in a large pie dish. Spread half of the marinade over the ribs to cover all surfaces. Cover and stand 30 minutes.

2 Preheat the oven to 220°C (425°F, gas mark 7). Place the ribs on a rack in a baking dish and pour some water under the rack to prevent drippings from charring. Bake for 30 minutes. Reduce heat to 180°C (350°F, gas mark 4) and bake for 40 minutes, brushing well with remaining marinade every 15 minutes to glaze. Serve immediately.

i

preparation time
10 minutes, plus 30 minutes marinating

cooking time
1 hour 10 minutes

nutritional value per serve
fat: 15.8 g
carbohydrate: 3.4 g
protein: 24.5 g

fried noodles with chicken stir-fry

ingredients

200 g (7 oz) wheat noodles
250 g (8 oz) chicken breast fillets
   cut into 5 cm wide strips
1/2 teaspoon salt
1/2 teaspoon five-spice powder
2 tablespoons oil
1 clove garlic, halved
1 red capsicum (pepper), deseeded
   and cut into strips
4 mushrooms, sliced
4 spring onions (green onions)
2 baby bok choy (pak choi), leaves
   separated
425 g (14 oz) can baby corn, drained
1 tablespoon dry sherry
2 teaspoons cornflour
1 tablespoon oyster sauce
serves 4

preparation time
15 minutes

cooking time
6 minutes

nutritional value
per serve
fat: 3.9 g
carbohydrate: 15 g
protein: 6.5 g

1 Soak wheat noodles in hot water for 5 minutes, drain well. Sprinkle chicken strips with salt and five-spice powder.

2 Heat the wok, add 2 teaspoons of oil. Place in the noodles and stir-fry until hot and coloured a little. Remove and keep hot.

3 Add 2 teaspoons of oil to the wok, add garlic and fry for 1 minute then remove. Add chicken and stir-fry for 2 minutes. Remove and keep hot.

4 Add more oil to the wok if needed. Add capsicums, mushrooms and spring onions, and stir-fry for 1 minute. Toss in bok choy and baby corn.

5 In a small bowl, combine sherry and cornflour until smooth, add oyster sauce. Return chicken to the wok and toss, stir in blended sauce and toss well to distribute. Stir-fry for 1–2 minutes to thicken and reheat. Pile over hot noodles and serve immediately.

chicken laksa

ingredients

$^1/_3$ cup (90 ml, 3 fl oz) vegetable oil
4 small fresh red chillies, finely chopped
1 stalk fresh lemon grass, finely
    chopped or $^1/_2$ teaspoon dried lemon
    grass, soaked in hot water until soft
3 cloves garlic, crushed
2 tablespoons finely grated fresh ginger
1 teaspoon ground cumin
1 teaspoon ground turmeric
6 candlenuts or unsalted macadamia nuts
$^1/_4$ teaspoon shrimp paste
1 litre ($1^2/_3$ pints) coconut milk
4 boneless chicken breast fillets, cut
    into 2 cm cubes
2 tablespoons chopped fresh coriander
375 g (12 oz) rice noodles, cooked
125 g (4 oz) bean sprouts
125 g (4 oz) fried tofu, sliced
serves 4

i

preparation time
20 minutes

cooking time
15 minutes

**nutritional value
per serve**
fat: 14.9 g
carbohydrate: 4 g
protein: 10.5 g

1 Into a food processor place 2 tablespoons oil, chillies, lemon grass, garlic, ginger, cumin, turmeric, candlenuts or macadamia nuts and shrimp paste and process to make a smooth paste.

2 In a large saucepan, heat the remaining oil over a medium heat, add paste and cook, stirring, for 2 minutes or until fragrant. Stir in coconut milk and simmer, stirring occasionally, for 15 minutes or until mixture thickens slightly.

3 Add chicken and coriander and simmer, stirring occasionally, for 15 minutes longer or until chicken is tender. To serve, divide rice noodles between serving bowls, top with bean sprouts and tofu, pour over coconut milk mixture and serve immediately.

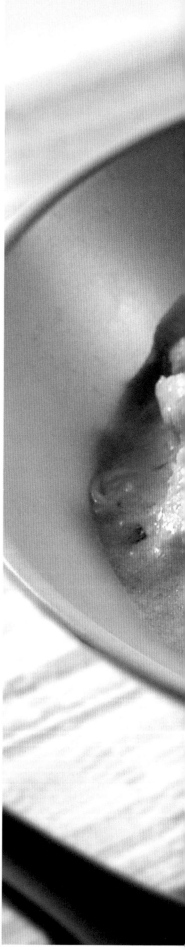

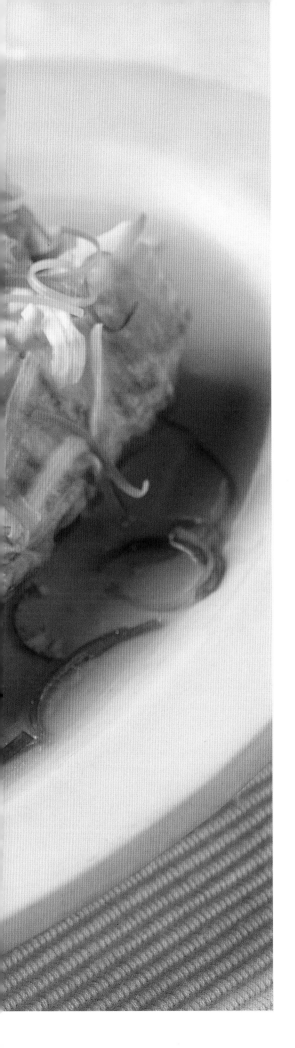

seafood

chinese-style steamed grey mullet

ingredients

1 grey mullet, about 700 g (1 lb 7 oz),
  scaled and gutted
1/2 teaspoon salt
1 tablespoon vegetable oil
1 tablespoon light soy sauce
1 large carrot, cut into fine strips
4 spring onions (green onions),
  cut into fine strips
1 tablespoon grated fresh root ginger
1 tablespoon sesame oil (optional)
fresh coriander to garnish

serves 2

1 In a small bowl, combine salt, vegetable oil and soy sauce. Make 4 deep slashes along each side of the fish, and rub inside and out with the sauce mixture. Cover and place in the refrigerator for 30 minutes.

i

preparation time
10 minutes,
plus 30 minutes
refrigeration

cooking time
20 minutes

**nutritional value
per serve**
fat: 8.8 g
carbohydrate: 0.8 g
protein: 15.4 g

2 Spread half the carrot, spring onions and ginger in the centre of a large piece of foil. Place the fish on top, then sprinkle with the remaining vegetables and ginger and any remaining oil mixture.

3 Loosely fold over the foil and seal. Transfer the fish to a steamer or a rack set over a roasting tin half filled with water. Cover the steamer tightly with a lid or the roasting pan with foil. Cook for 20 minutes or until the fish is firm and cooked through. Put the sesame oil, if using, into a small saucepan and heat. Drizzle over the fish and garnish with coriander.

tiger prawn, snow pea and mango stir-fry

ingredients

400 g (13 oz) green tiger prawns, peeled
2 tablespoons vegetable oil
1¹/₂ tablespoons finely grated fresh root
   ginger
300 g (10 oz) snow peas (mangetout)
bunch of spring onions (green onions),
   sliced
1 large ripe mango, peeled and thinly
   sliced
2 tablespoons light soy sauce
serves 4

1 Cut a slit along the back of each prawn with a sharp knife and remove any thin black vein.

2 Heat the wok on a high heat, add oil, ginger and prawns and stir-fry for 2 minutes or until the prawns are just turning pink. Add the snow peas and spring onions and stir-fry for a further minute to soften slightly. Stir in the mango and soy sauce and stir-fry for 1 minute to heat through. Serve with steamed rice.

i

preparation time
15 minutes

cooking time
5 minutes

**nutritional value
per serve**
fat: 3.6 g
carbohydrate: 4.2 g
protein: 8.6 g

1 In a bowl, combine lime juice, rice wine and garlic. Add scallops and set aside for 15 minutes. In a wok, heat the sesame oil. Add ginger, spring onions, mushrooms and capsicum. Stir-fry for about 3 minutes until ginger is fragrant.

2 Add scallops and marinade, and stir-fry for 3 minutes until scallops have become opaque. Add soy sauce and pepper to taste. In a cup, combine cornflour and water to a paste. Add paste to wok and cook while stirring until sauce thickens slightly. Serve immediately with steamed white rice.

ginger scallop stir-fry

ingredients

2 tablespoons fresh lime juice
2 tablespoons rice wine
1 clove garlic, crushed
250 g (8 oz) fresh scallops
1 tablespoon sesame oil
2 teaspoons finely grated
   fresh root ginger
4 spring onions (green onions),
   cut diagonally into 2 cm lengths
90 g (3 oz) button mushrooms, sliced
½ red capsicum (pepper), diced
2 teaspoons soy sauce
pepper
1 teaspoon cornflour
2 tablespoons water
serves 4

i

preparation time
20 minutes

cooking time
8 minutes

**nutritional value
per serve**
fat: 3.7 g
carbohydrate: 2 g
protein: 6.4 g

southeast asian pan-fried prawns

ingredients

500 g (1 lb) green prawns
3 small red chillies, deseeded and
    chopped
2 cloves garlic, chopped
2.5 cm piece fresh root ginger, chopped
1 spring onion (green onion), chopped
2 tablespoons peanut oil
1 onion, chopped
2 tomatoes, quartered
1 teaspoon sugar
salt
serves 4

preparation time
25 minutes

cooking time
8 minutes

**nutritional value
per serve**
fat: 4.1 g
carbohydrate: 1.9 g
protein: 10.2 g

1 Shell the prawns, leaving the tails attached. Cut a slit along the back of each prawn with a sharp knife and remove the thin black vein. Rinse well and refrigerate. In a food processor, blend the chillies, garlic, ginger and spring onion to a paste.

2 Heat a wok over a high heat, add oil and onion and fry for 2 minutes to soften slightly. Add paste and stir-fry for 1 minute to release the flavours. Add prawns and tomatoes, mixing thoroughly, then sprinkle over sugar and salt to taste. Stir-fry for 3–5 minutes, until prawns turn pink and are cooked through.

thai fish cakes with peanut dipping sauce

ingredients

350 g (11½ oz) skinless cod fillets
1 tablespoon thai red curry paste
1 tablespoon thai fish sauce
2 tablespoons cornflour
1 medium egg, beaten
1 spring onion (green onion), finely chopped
60 g (2 oz) fine green beans, cut into 5 mm lengths
peanut oil for shallow-frying

dipping sauce

2 tablespoons sugar
juice of 1 lime
1 clove garlic, finely chopped
1 cm piece fresh root ginger, finely chopped
1 tablespoon roughly crushed roasted salted peanuts
1 small red chilli, deseeded and finely chopped
2 tablespoons light soy sauce

serves 4

preparation time
20 minutes

cooking time
16 minutes

nutritional value per serve
fat: 16.9 g
carbohydrate: 7.5 g
protein: 9.8 g

1 In a food processor, finely mince the cod fillets. Add red curry paste, fish sauce, cornflour and egg. Blend briefly or stir until mixed. Transfer to a bowl and combine with spring onions and beans.

2 Lightly oil your hands (it's quite sticky), then divide mixture and shape into 8 patties. In a bowl, combine sugar and lime juice, stirring until sugar dissolves. Stir in garlic, ginger, peanuts, chilli and soy sauce. Set aside.

3 Heat 1 cm of oil in a large frying pan over a medium to high heat, then fry half of the fish cakes for 3–4 minutes on each side, until golden. Drain on kitchen paper, then cook remaining cakes. Serve with dipping sauce.

baked cod with ginger and spring onions

ingredients

oil for greasing
500 g (1 lb) piece cod fillet
1 tablespoon light soy sauce
1 tablespoon rice wine or medium-dry
  sherry
1 teaspoon sesame oil
salt
3 spring onions (green onions),
  shredded and cut into 2.5 cm pieces,
  white and green parts separated
2.5 cm piece fresh root ginger,
  finely chopped

serves 4

1 Preheat the oven to 190°C (375°F, gas mark 5). Line a shallow baking tray with a piece of lightly greased foil to come past the sides of the baking tray. Place the cod on the tray, skin-side down. Pour over the soy sauce, rice wine or sherry, oil and salt to taste, then sprinkle over white spring onion and ginger.

2 Loosely wrap the foil over the fish, folding the edges together to seal. Bake for 20–25 minutes, until cooked through and tender. Unwrap the parcel, transfer the fish to a serving plate and sprinkle over spring onions.

preparation time
10 minutes

cooking time
25 minutes

**nutritional value
per serve**
fat: 1.4 g
carbohydrate: 0.6 g
protein: 15.1 g

seafood with oyster mushrooms

ingredients

125 g (4 oz) small calamari (squid) hoods
8 baby octopus
8 medium-sized green prawns, shelled
  and deveined
155 g (5 oz) fresh scallops
2 teaspoons vegetable oil
250 g (8 oz) oyster mushrooms
6 spring onions (green onions), chopped
freshly ground black pepper

marinade

3 tablespoons chopped fresh coriander
2 cloves garlic, crushed
4 tablespoons worcestershire sauce
1/3 cup (90 ml, 3 fl oz) soy sauce
2 tablespoons sweet chilli sauce

serves 4-6

1 Cut down the length of the squid's hood and open out. Score the inside surface into a diamond pattern taking care not to cut right through to the flesh. Clean the baby octopus by cutting off the head below the eyes and discard. Push out and remove the beak located in the centre of the tentacles. Wash well.

2 In a bowl, combine all marinade ingredients and add squid, octopus, prawns and scallops. Toss to coat with marinade, cover and refrigerate for 2–3 hours.

3 Drain seafood and reserve the marinade. Heat a wok until very hot, add oil swirling to coat base and sides. Add squid and octopus and stir-fry for 2 minutes then add prawns and scallops. Stir-fry for 1 minute.

4 Add mushrooms, spring onions and 3 tablespoons reserved marinade and stir-fry for 2 minutes more. Season to taste with black pepper. Transfer to a serving dish and serve immediately.

preparation time
15 minutes, plus
2-3 hours
marinating

cooking time
5 minutes

**nutritional value
per serve**
fat: 1.5 g
carbohydrate: 3.2 g
protein: 10.7 g

lime fish with noodles

ingredients

2 teaspoons vegetable oil

3 spring onions (green onions), chopped

1 stalk fresh lemon grass, chopped or
$^1/_2$ teaspoon dried lemon grass,
soaked in hot water until soft

1 fresh red chilli, chopped

750 g (1$^1/_2$ lb) firm white fish fillets, cut
into thick strips

2 tablespoons lime juice

315 g (10 oz) fresh rice noodles

$^1/_2$ bunch (250 g, 8 oz) bok choy
(pak choi), chopped

4 tablespoons water

2 tablespoons soy sauce

2 teaspoons white miso

serves 4

preparation time
10 minutes

cooking time
5 minutes

**nutritional value
per serve**
fat: 1.9 g
carbohydrate: 5.2 g
protein: 11.3 g

1 Heat wok over a high heat, add the oil, spring onions, lemon grass and chilli and stir-fry for 1 minute. Add fish and lime juice and stir-fry for 2 minutes or until fish is almost cooked. Remove fish mixture from wok and set aside.

2 Add noodles, bok choy, water, soy sauce and miso to wok and stir-fry for 2 minutes. Return fish mixture to wok and stir-fry for 1 minute or until heated through

oriental-style salmon fillets

ingredients

4 skinless salmon fillets
2 tablespoons vegetable oil
2 tablespoons light soy sauce
2 tablespoons clear honey
25 g (1 oz) stem ginger, drained and
    finely chopped
2 spring onions (green onions), cut into
    long strips
finely grated rind (zest) and juice
    of $^1/_2$ lime
black pepper
lime wedges to serve
serves 4

preparation time
5 minutes,
plus 30 minutes
marinating

cooking time
8 minutes

**nutritional value
per serve**
fat: 11 g
carbohydrate: 8.5 g
protein: 13.7 g

1 Place the salmon fillets in a shallow non-metallic dish. Mix together the oil, soy sauce, honey, ginger, spring onions, lime rind and juice and seasoning. Pour over the fillets and turn to coat. Cover and marinate in the refrigerator for 30 minutes to 1 hour.

2 Preheat the grill to high. Lightly oil a baking tray. Lift the fillets and spring onions out of the marinade and place on the baking tray. Brush the fillets with a little of the marinade, then cook for 3 minutes. Turn over, brush with more of the marinade and grill for 3–5 minutes until cooked through. Garnish with lime wedges.

fragrant salmon stir-fry

ingredients

250 g (8 oz) skinless salmon fillets
1¹⁄₂ tablespoons peanut or sunflower oil
1 tablespoon chilled butter, cubed
marinade
1 stalk lemon grass
1 tablespoon soy sauce
¹⁄₂ cup (125 ml, 4 fl oz) orange juice
1 tablespoon chopped fresh dill
1 tablespoon chopped fresh basil
1 teaspoon grated fresh root ginger
1 clove garlic, crushed
salt and black pepper
serves 2

preparation time
10 minutes,
2 hours marinating

cooking time
10 minutes

**nutritional value
per serve**
fat: 12.6 g
carbohydrate: 2.5 g
protein: 11.2 g

1 Peel the outer layer from the lemon grass stalk, then finely chop the lower white bulbous part. In a bowl, combine lemon grass, soy sauce, orange juice, ¹⁄₂

tablespoon dill, ¹⁄₂ tablespoon basil, ginger, garlic and seasoning. Cut the salmon fillet into strips 2.5 cm wide and 7.5 cm long. Arrange strips in a shallow non-metallic dish and pour over marinade, turning strips to coat. Cover and refrigerate for 2 hours.

2 Remove salmon from dish and set aside the marinade. Pat salmon dry. Heat the oil in a large, heavy-based frying pan over a medium to high heat, add salmon and cook for 2 minutes on each side.

3 Arrange salmon on serving plates. Pour reserved marinade into the frying pan, bring to the boil and simmer for 2 minutes. Whisk in butter, a cube at a time. Spoon sauce over the salmon and sprinkle over remaining dill and basil.

singapore noodles with prawns and ham

ingredients

250 g (8 oz) fresh stir-fry rice noodles
3 tablespoons vegetable oil
1 red chilli, deseeded and finely chopped
4 tablespoons singapore fried
   noodle paste
2 tablespoons white-wine vinegar
1 tablespoon sugar
1 red capsicum (pepper), deseeded and
   thinly sliced
175 g (6 oz) button mushrooms, sliced
225 g (7$\frac{1}{2}$ oz) cooked ham, cut into strips
100 g (3$\frac{1}{2}$ oz) frozen peas
225 g (7$\frac{1}{2}$ oz) can water chestnuts,
   drained and halved
225 g (8 oz) green prawns, peeled
4 spring onions (green onions),
   finely sliced

serves 4

i

preparation time
35 minutes

cooking time
10 minutes

**nutritional value
per serve**
fat: 4.9 g
carbohydrate: 7.4 g
protein: 7.4 g

1 Prepare the noodles. Heat the wok or heavy-based frying pan until very hot. Add oil, chilli, fried noodle paste, vinegar and sugar and cook for 1–2 minutes, stirring constantly to release the flavours. Add capsicum and mushrooms and stir-fry for 3 minutes or until vegetables have softened.

2 Add ham, peas, water chestnuts and prawns and stir-fry for 2–3 minutes until the prawns turn pink. Add spring onions and noodles. Cook for 1 minute, stirring, or until prawns are cooked through and everything is hot.

vegetarian

curried vegetables

ingredients

2¹/₂ tablespoons vegetable oil

2 spring onions (green onions), sliced thinly

3 cloves garlic, crushed

3 tablespoons curry powder

2 teaspoons shrimp paste (optional)

2 stalks lemon grass, trimmed and thinly sliced

2 dried red chillies, chopped

1 cup (250 ml, 8 fl oz) stock

1 cup (250 ml, 8 fl oz) coconut milk

1 tablespoon fish sauce

2 lime leaves or strips of lime or lemon peel

115 g (4 oz) carrots, cut diagonally into 3¹/₂ cm pieces

255 g (8 oz) potatoes, peeled and quartered

115 g (4 oz) green beans, topped and tailed

1 eggplant (aubergine), cut 1¹/₂ cm cubes
salt

serves 4

i

preparation time
15 minutes

cooking time
15 minutes

nutritional value per serve
fat: 7.4 g
carbohydrate: 5.1 g
protein: 1.9 g

1 Heat oil in a heavy-based pan, add spring onions and garlic to saute until just golden. Add curry powder, shrimp paste if desired, lemon grass and chillies and cook about 6 minutes. Add stock, coconut milk, fish sauce and lime leaves or citrus peel. Cover and bring to boil.

2 Reduce heat to medium, add carrots, potatoes, beans and eggplant, part-cover and simmer about 15 minutes until vegetables are tender and liquid has reduced.

spring vegetables in spiced coconut curry

ingredients

1 stalk lemon grass, peeled and white
    part finely chopped
2 tablespoons vegetable oil
1 cm piece fresh root ginger, chopped
1 onion, finely chopped
1 clove garlic, finely chopped
1 teaspoon turmeric
225 g (7$\frac{1}{2}$ oz) potatoes,
    cut into 2 cm chunks
2 carrots, thickly sliced
400 ml (13 fl oz) can coconut milk
2 bay leaves
1 red chilli, deseeded and finely chopped
salt
125 g (4 oz) baby sweetcorn, cobs,
    fresh or frozen
170 g (5$\frac{1}{2}$ oz) fine green beans
2 zucchini (courgettes), thickly sliced
2 tablespoons chopped fresh coriander
serves 4

1 Heat the oil in a large, heavy-based saucepan. Add lemon grass, ginger, onion and garlic and fry for 5 minutes or until the onion and garlic have softened. Stir in turmeric, potatoes and carrots, then add the coconut milk, bay leaves, chilli and salt. Bring to the boil, reduce the heat and simmer, partly covered, for 10 minutes, stirring occasionally.

2 Add sweetcorn and beans and simmer, partly covered, for 10 minutes. Add the zucchini and cook for a further 10 minutes or until all the vegetables are tender. Remove the bay leaves and garnish with coriander just before serving.

i

preparation time
20 minutes

cooking time
35 minutes

**nutritional value
per serve**
fat: 8.8 g
carbohydrate: 6.1 g
protein: 1.9 g

green vegetable stir-fry with sesame seeds

ingredients

2 tablespoons sesame seeds

2 tablespoons peanut oil

1 clove garlic, roughly chopped

2.5 cm piece fresh root ginger, finely chopped

150 g (5 oz) broccoli, cut into very small florets, peel and slice the thick stems

2 zucchini (courgettes), halved lengthways and finely sliced

170 g (5¹/₂ oz) snow peas (mangetout)

1 tablespoon rice wine or medium-dry sherry

1 tablespoon dark soy sauce

1 tablespoon oyster sauce

serves 4

ℹ

preparation time
10 minutes

cooking time
15 minutes

nutritional value per serve
fat: 7.8 g
carbohydrate: 2.9 g
protein: 3.3 g

1 Heat a wok, add sesame seeds and dry-fry for 2 minutes until golden, shaking the wok frequently. Remove and set aside. Add oil to the hot wok, then add garlic and ginger and stir-fry over a medium heat for 1–2 minutes until softened. Add broccoli and stir-fry for a further 2–3 minutes.

2 Add the zucchini and snow peas and stir-fry for 3 minutes. Pour over the rice wine or sherry and sizzle for a minute. Add the soy and oyster sauces, mix well and stir-fry for 2 minutes. Sprinkle over toasted sesame seeds just before serving.

split lentil dhal with ginger and coriander

ingredients

200 g (7 oz) dried split red lentils
$1/2$ teaspoon turmeric
1 tablespoon vegetable oil
1 cm piece fresh root ginger, finely
  chopped
1 teaspoon cumin seeds
1 teaspoon ground coriander
salt and black pepper
4 tablespoons chopped fresh coriander
$1/2$ teaspoon paprika
extra coriander to garnish
serves 4

1 Rinse the lentils and drain well, then place in a large saucepan with 850 ml (1½ pints) of water. Bring to the boil, skimming off any scum, then stir in turmeric. Reduce the heat and partly cover the pan. Simmer for 30–35 minutes, until thickened, stirring occasionally.

2 Heat the oil in a small frying pan. Add ginger and cumin seeds and fry for 30 seconds or until cumin seeds start to pop. Stir in ground coriander and fry for 1 minute.

3 Season the lentils with salt and pepper, then add the toasted spices. Stir in the chopped coriander, mixing well. Transfer to a serving dish and garnish with the paprika and coriander leaves.

i

preparation time
10 minutes

cooking time
40 minutes

nutritional value per serve
fat: 9.7 g
carbohydrate: 32 g
protein: 20.9 g

herbed rice noodles with asparagus and peanuts

ingredients

3 tablespoons rice vinegar

1 tablespoon sugar

1 small spanish onion, finely sliced into rings

255 g (8 oz) dried rice noodles

2 bunches of asparagus

a handful fresh mint, chopped

a handful fresh coriander, chopped

1 continental cucumber, peeled, seeded and thinly sliced

6 spring onions (green onions), finely sliced

3 roma tomatoes, finely diced

120 g (4 oz) roasted peanuts, lightly crushed

juice of 2 limes

2 teaspoons fish sauce

2 teaspoons olive oil

1/2 teaspoon chilli flakes

serves 4

preparation time
20 minutes, plus
1 hour marination

cooking tme
4 minutes

**nutritional value
per serve**
fat: 3.8 g
carbohydrate: 6 g
protein: 3 g

1 Whisk the rice vinegar and sugar together and pour over the onion rings. Allow to marinate for 1 hour, tossing frequently. Cook rice noodles in boiling water for 1–2 minutes then drain immediately and rinse under cold water. Cut into a manageable length with kitchen scissors.

2 Peel the tough skin off the lower third of the asparagus stalk with a potato peeler, then cut into 2 cm lengths. Simmer asparagus in salted water for 2 minutes until bright green and crisp-tender. Rinse in cold water to refresh.

3 Toss the noodles with the onion and vinegar mixture while still warm. Add asparagus, mint, coriander, cucumber, spring onions, tomatoes and roasted peanuts and toss thoroughly. In a small bowl, whisk the lime juice, fish sauce, oil and chilli flakes together and drizzle over the noodle salad. Serve at room temperature.

vegetable stir-fry with noodles

ingredients

250 g (8 oz) broad ribbon egg noodles
2 tablespoons sunflower oil
1 clove garlic, sliced
2 carrots, thinly sliced diagonally
150 g (5 oz) green beans, halved
150 g (5 oz) broccoli florets
1 red capsicum (pepper), deseeded and
 cut into thin strips
4 spring onions (green onions), thinly
 sliced diagonally

sauce

4 tablespoons smooth peanut butter
1 tablespoon tomato purée
1 tablespoon balsamic vinegar
sea salt and freshly ground black pepper
fresh coriander, chopped
lemon wedges, to serve

serves 4

1 Cook the noodles. In a bowl, combine the peanut butter, tomato purée, balsamic vinegar and seasoning with about 4 tablespoons of cold water. Set aside.

2 Heat a wok or large frying pan until very hot. Add oil, garlic, carrots and green beans and stir-fry for 2 minutes, until lightly coloured. Add broccoli and stir-fry for 2–3 minutes or until softened. Add capsicum and spring onions, then cook for a further 1 minute.

3 Add the sauce, 1/2 cup (125 ml, 4 fl oz) water and noodles. Combine well and stir-fry for 4–5 minutes or until everything is hot. Garnish with fresh coriander and serve with lemon wedges.

preparation time
25 minutes

cooking time
15 minutes

nutritional value per serve
fat: 9.1 g
carbohydrate: 15 g
protein: 6.5 g

root vegetable curry

ingredients

1 tablespoon olive oil
1 onion, chopped
1 green chilli, deseeded and finely chopped
1 clove garlic, finely chopped
2.5 cm piece fresh root ginger, finely chopped
2 tablespoons plain flour
2 teaspoons ground coriander
2 teaspoons ground cumin
2 teaspoons turmeric
300 ml (10 fl oz) vegetable stock
200 ml (7 fl oz) can tomato puree
750 g (1½ lb) mixed root vegetables (potato, sweet potato, celeriac, swede etc), cubed
2 carrots, thinly sliced
black pepper
fresh coriander, chopped to garnish
serves 4

i

preparation time
20 minutes

cooking time
55 minutes

nutritional value per serve
fat: 1.4 g
carbohydrate: 9 g
protein: 1.8 g

1 Heat the oil in a large saucepan. Add the onion, chilli, garlic and ginger and cook for 5 minutes or until softened, stirring occasionally. Stir in flour, coriander, cumin and turmeric and cook gently, stirring, for 1 minute to release the flavours.

2 Gradually stir in stock, then add tomato puree, root vegetables and carrots, season with black pepper and mix well. Bring to the boil, stirring, then cover, reduce heat and simmer for 45 minutes or until the vegetables are tender, stirring occasionally. Garnish with fresh coriander.

tofu and bok choy

ingredients

315 g (10 oz) firm tofu, cut into 2 cm cubes
60 g (2 oz) walnuts, roughly chopped
1 tablespoon finely grated fresh ginger
1 tablespoon chopped fresh coriander
4 tablespoons japanese soy sauce
1 teaspoon sesame oil
2 tablespoons vegetable oil
1 bunch (about 500 g, 1 lb) bok choy
   (pak choi), chopped
1 bunch (500 g, 1 lb) chinese broccoli,
   chopped
1 tablespoon oyster sauce
1 tablespoon sweet chilli sauce
serves 4

i

preparation time
10 minutes,
plus 2 hours
marination

cooking time
10 minutes

**nutritional value
per serve**
fat: 6.9 g
carbohydrate: 1.6 g
protein: 5.2 g

1 In a bowl, combine tofu, walnuts, ginger, coriander, soy sauce and sesame oil. Cover and marinate at room temperature for 2 hours. Drain tofu and walnuts and reserve marinade.

2 Heat 1 tablespoon vegetable oil in a wok over a medium heat. Add bok choy and broccoli and stir-fry for 3 minutes or until just tender. Remove to a serving platter and keep warm.

3 Heat remaining oil in wok, add tofu and walnuts and stir-fry for 5 minutes or until tofu is golden. Add reserved marinade and oyster and chilli sauces, then stir-fry for 2 minutes. Place on top of vegetables. Serve immediately.

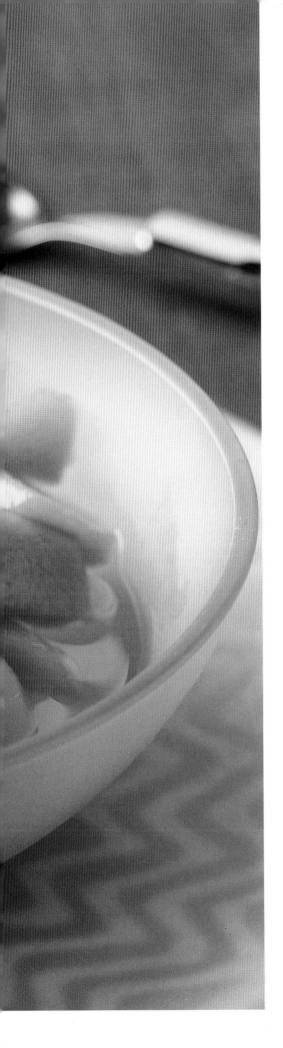

desserts

mango cake with nutmeg cream

ingredients

160 g (5¹/₂ oz) unsalted, roasted
  macadamia nuts
3 large mangoes
255 g (8 oz) butter
250 g (8 oz) castor sugar
1 teaspoon vanilla essence
4 large eggs
250 g (8 oz) plain flour
1¹/₂ teaspoons baking powder
80 g (3 oz) roasted macadamia nuts,
  chopped
icing sugar
2 cups (500 ml, 16 fl oz) pure cream
1 teaspoon nutmeg
1 mango, sliced, for serving
serves 6

1 Preheat the oven to 180°C (350°F, gas mark 4) and butter a 22 cm non-stick cake tin.

2 Crush 160 g (5¹/₃ oz) roasted macadamia nuts in a food processor and set aside. Peel the mangoes and dice the flesh, saving as much juice as possible. Reserve about ¹/₂ cup mango dices and purée the remainder (about 1 cup of mango purée).

3 Cream the softened butter and vanilla essence with ¹/₂ cup (125 g, 4 oz) sugar and beat until thick and pale. Add remaining sugar and beat until all sugar has been added. Add the eggs, one at a time, and beat well after each addition.

4 In a separate bowl, mix the crushed nuts, flour and baking powder together. Fold in the flour mixture, stirring well to combine. Add the mango purée and mix gently.

5 Spoon the batter into the tin. Sprinkle over chopped macadamia nuts and reserved diced mango and swirl through Bake at 170°C (325°F) for 1 hour, remove from the oven and cool in the tin. When cool, remove cake from the tin. Dredge with icing sugar. In a bowl, whip the cream and nutmeg together until the cream is thick and fragrant. Serve alongside the cake with some mango slices.

i

preparation time
15 minutes

cooking time
1 hour

**nutritional value
per serve**
fat: 26.5 g
carbohydrate: 22 g
protein: 4 g

rum and lime banana fritters

ingredients

4 bananas
juice of 1 lime
2 teaspoons castor sugar
1 tablespoon dark rum
oil for deep-frying
batter
100 g (3½ oz) self-raising flour
pinch of salt
150 ml (5 fl oz) water
2 tablespoons sesame seeds

serves 4

1 Peel each banana and cut in half crossways, then slice lengthways to make quarters. Place the banana quarters, lime juice, sugar and rum in a deep, non-metallic dish and mix gently. Cover and set aside for 30 minutes to marinate.

2 Sift the flour and salt into a mixing bowl. Pour in 150 ml (5 fl oz) water and whisk to form a smooth, thick batter. Stir in the sesame seeds and set aside.

3 Heat 5 cm of oil in a wok or large frying pan until smoking hot. Coat the banana pieces thoroughly in the batter. Fry for 5 minutes or until golden brown. Turn over and cook for 2 minutes to brown the other side. Drain on kitchen towels.

preparation time
10 minutes, plus
30 minutes
marination

cooking time
15 minutes

nutritional value per serve
fat: 29.3 g
carbohydrate: 19 g
protein: 2.6 g

baked passion fruit custards

ingredients

4 large eggs, beaten
4 tablespoons castor sugar
150 ml (5 fl oz) coconut milk
pinch of salt
2 passion fruit

serves 4

i

preparation time
10 minutes

cooking time
40 minutes

nutritional value per serve
fat: 11.1 g
carbohydrate: 15 g
protein: 6.9 g

1 Preheat the oven to 180°C (350°F, gas mark 4). Whisk together the eggs, sugar, coconut milk and salt until smooth, then pour into 4 ramekins.

2 Halve 1 passion fruit, scoop out the pulp and seeds and divide between the 4 custard-filled ramekins. Place ramekins in a deep roasting tin.

3 Pour boiling water into the roasting tin to three-quarters of the way up the sides of the ramekins. Bake the custards for 40 minutes. Serve warm or cold with the pulp and seeds from the remaining passion fruit spooned over the top.

oriental
fruit
salad

ingredients

3 stalks lemon grass
60 g (2 oz) castor sugar
1 small rock melon (cantaloupe)
1 mango
425 g (14 oz) can lychees, drained
fresh mint leaves to garnish
serves 4

preparation time
30 minutes,
plus 20 minutes
cooling and 30
minutes chilling

cooking time
5 minutes

**nutritional value
per serve**
fat: 0.2 g
carbohydrate: 13 g
protein: 0.7 g

1 Peel the outer layers from the lemon grass stalks and finely chop the lower white bulbous parts. In a pan, place the lemon grass, sugar and 100 ml (3½ fl oz) water. Simmer, stirring, for 5 minutes or until sugar dissolves, then bring to the boil. Remove from heat and leave to cool for 20 minutes. Refrigerate for 30 minutes.

2 Halve the melon and scrape out the seeds. Cut into wedges, remove skin and cut the flesh into small chunks. Slice off the two fat sides of the mango close to the stone. Cut a criss-cross pattern across the flesh, of each piece, then push the skin up to expose the cubes of flesh and cut them off. Place the melon, mango and lychees in serving bowls. Strain the lemon grass syrup and pour over the fruit. Decorate with mint.

glossary

al dente: Italian term to describe pasta and rice that are cooked until tender but still firm to the bite.

bake blind: to bake pastry cases without their fillings. Line the raw pastry case with greaseproof paper and fill with raw rice or dried beans to prevent collapsed sides and puffed base. Remove paper and fill 5 minutes before completion of cooking time.

baste: to spoon hot cooking liquid over food at intervals during cooking to moisten and flavour it.

beat: to make a mixture smooth with rapid and regular motions using a spatula, wire whisk or electric mixer; to make a mixture light and smooth by enclosing air.

beurre manié: equal quantities of butter and flour mixed together to a smooth paste and stirred bit by bit into a soup, stew or sauce while on the heat to thicken. Stop adding when desired thickness results.

bind: to add egg or a thick sauce to hold ingredients together when cooked.

blanch: to plunge some foods into boiling water for less than a minute and immediately plunge into iced water. This is to brighten the colour of some vegetables; to remove skin from tomatoes and nuts.

blend: to mix 2 or more ingredients thoroughly together; do not confuse with blending in an electric blender.

boil: to cook in a liquid brought to boiling point and kept there.

boiling point: when bubbles rise continually and break over the entire surface of the liquid, reaching a temperature of 100°C (212°F). In some cases food is held at this high temperature for a few seconds then heat is turned to low for slower cooking. See simmer.

bouquet garni: a bundle of several herbs tied together with string for easy removal, placed into pots of stock, soups and stews for flavour. A few sprigs of fresh thyme, parsley and bay leaf are used. Can be purchased in sachet form for convenience.

caramelise: to heat sugar in a heavy-based pan until it liquefies and develops a caramel colour. Vegetables such as blanched carrots and sautéed onions may be sprinkled with sugar and caramelised.

chill: to place in the refrigerator or stir over ice until cold.

clarify: to make a liquid clear by removing sediments and impurities. To melt fat and remove any sediment.

coat: to dust or roll food items in flour to cover the surface before the food is cooked. Also, to coat in flour, egg and breadcrumbs.

cool: to stand at room temperature until some or all heat is removed, eg, cool a little, cool completely.

cream: to make creamy and fluffy by working the mixture with the back of a wooden spoon, usually refers to creaming butter and sugar or margarine. May also be creamed with an electric mixer.

croutons: small cubes of bread, toasted or fried, used as an addition to salads or as a garnish to soups and stews.

crudite: raw vegetable sticks served with a dipping sauce.

crumb: to coat foods in flour, egg and breadcrumbs to form a protective coating for foods which are fried. Also adds flavour, texture and enhances appearance.

cube: to cut into small pieces with six even sides, eg, cubes of meat.

cut in: to combine fat and flour using 2 knives scissor fashion or with a pastry blender, to make pastry.

deglaze: to dissolve dried out cooking juices left on the base and sides of a roasting dish or frying pan. Add a little water, wine or stock, scrape and stir over heat until dissolved. Resulting liquid is used to make a flavoursome gravy or added to a sauce or casserole.

degrease: to skim fat from the surface of cooking liquids, eg, stocks, soups, casseroles.

dice: to cut into small cubes.

dredge: to heavily coat with icing sugar, sugar, flour or cornflour.

dressing: a mixture added to completed dishes to add moisture and flavour, eg, salads, cooked vegetables.

drizzle: to pour in a fine thread-like stream moving over a surface.

egg wash: beaten egg with milk or water used to brush over pastry, bread dough or biscuits to give a sheen and golden brown colour.

essence: a strong flavouring liquid, usually made by distillation. Only a few drops are needed to flavour.

fillet: a piece of prime meat, fish or poultry which is boneless or has all bones removed.

flake: to separate cooked fish into flakes, removing any bones and skin, using 2 forks.

flame: to ignite warmed alcohol over food or to pour into a pan with food, ignite then serve.

flute: to make decorative indentations around the pastry rim before baking.

fold in: combining of a light, whisked or creamed mixture with other ingredients. Add a portion of the other ingredients at a time and mix using a gentle circular motion, over and under the mixture so that air will not be lost. Use a silver spoon or spatula.

glaze: to brush or coat food with a liquid that will give the finished product a glossy appearance, and on baked products, a golden brown colour.

grease: to rub the surface of a metal or heatproof dish with oil or fat, to prevent the food from sticking.

herbed butter: softened butter mixed with finely chopped fresh herbs and re-chilled. Used to serve on grilled meats and fish.

hors d'ouvre: small savoury foods served as an appetiser, popularly known today as 'finger food'.

infuse: to steep foods in a liquid until the liquid absorbs their flavour.

joint: to cut poultry and game into serving pieces by dividing at the joint.

julienne: to cut some food, eg, vegetables and processed meats into fine strips the length of matchsticks. Used for inclusion in salads or as a garnish to cooked dishes.

knead: to work a yeast dough in a pressing, stretching and folding motion with the heel of the hand until smooth and elastic to develop the gluten strands. Non-yeast doughs should be lightly and quickly handled as gluten development is not desired.

line: to cover the inside of a baking tin with paper for the easy removal of the cooked product from the baking tin.

macerate: to stand fruit in a syrup, liqueur or spirit to give added flavour.

marinade: a flavoured liquid, into which food is placed for some time to give it flavour and to tenderise. Marinades include an acid ingredient such as vinegar or wine, oil and seasonings.

mask: to evenly cover cooked food portions with a sauce, mayonnaise or savoury jelly.

pan-fry: to fry foods in a small amount of fat or oil, sufficient to coat the base of the pan.

parboil: to boil until partially cooked. The food is then finished by some other method.

pare: to peel the skin from vegetables and fruit. Peel is the popular term but pare is the name given to the knife used; paring knife.

pith: the white lining between the rind and flesh of oranges, grapefruit and lemons.

pit: to remove stones or seeds from olives, cherries, dates.

pitted: the olives, cherries, dates etc, with the stone removed, eg, purchase pitted dates.

poach: to simmer gently in enough hot liquid to almost cover the food so shape will be retained.

pound: to flatten meats with a meat mallet; to reduce to a paste or small particles with a mortar and pestle.

simmer: to cook in liquid just below boiling point at about 96ºC (205ºF) with small bubbles rising gently to the surface.

skim: to remove fat or froth from the surface of simmering food.

stock: the liquid produced when meat, poultry, fish or vegetables have been simmered in water to extract the flavour. Used as a base for soups, sauces, casseroles etc. Convenience stock products are available.

sweat: to cook sliced onions or vegetables, in a small amount of butter in a covered pan over low heat, to soften them and release flavour without colouring.

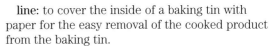

conversions

easurements differ from country to country, so it's important to understand what the differences are. This Measurements Guide gives you simple 'at-a-glance' information for using the recipes in this book, wherever you may be.

Cooking is not an exact science – minor variations in measurements won't make a difference to your cooking.

equipment

There is a difference in the size of measuring cups used internationally, but the difference is minimal (only 2–3 teaspoons). We use the Australian standard metric measurements in our recipes:

1 teaspoon ....5 ml   1 tablespoon....20 ml
1/2 cup......125 ml   1 cup.....250 ml
4 cups...1 litre

Measuring cups come in sets of one cup (250 ml), 1/2 cup (125 ml), 1/3 cup (80 ml) and 1/4 cup (60 ml). Use these for measuring liquids and certain dry ingredients.

Measuring spoons come in a set of four and should be used for measuring dry and liquid ingredients.

When using cup or spoon measures always make them level (unless the recipe indicates otherwise).

dry versus wet ingredients

While this system of measures is consistent for liquids, it's more difficult to quantify dry ingredients. For instance, one level cup equals: 200 g of brown sugar; 210 g of castor sugar; and 110 g of icing sugar.

When measuring dry ingredients such as flour, don't push the flour down or shake it into the cup. It is best just to spoon the flour in until it reaches the desired amount. When measuring liquids use a clear vessel indicating metric levels.

Always use medium eggs (55–60 g) when eggs are required in a recipe.

dry

metric (grams)	imperial (ounces)
30 g	1 oz
60 g	2 oz
90 g	3 oz
100 g	3 1/2 oz
125 g	4 oz
150 g	5 oz
185 g	6 oz
200 g	7 oz
250 g	8 oz
280 g	9 oz
315 g	10 oz
330 g	11 oz
370 g	12 oz
400 g	13 oz
440 g	14 oz
470 g	15 oz
500 g	16 oz (1 lb)
750 g	24 oz (1 1/2 lb)
1000 g (1 kg)	32 oz (2 lb)

liquids

metric (millilitres)	imperial (fluid ounces)
30 ml	1 fl oz
60 ml	2 fl oz
90 ml	3 fl oz
100 ml	3 1/2 fl oz
125 ml	4 fl oz
150 ml	5 fl oz
190 ml	6 fl oz
250 ml	8 fl oz
300 ml	10 fl oz
500 ml	16 fl oz
600 ml	20 fl oz (1 pint)*
1000 ml (1 litre)	32 fl oz

*Note: an American pint is 16 fl oz.

oven
Your oven should always be at the right temperature before placing the food in it to be cooked. Note that if your oven doesn't have a fan you may need to cook food for a little longer.

microwave
It is difficult to give an exact cooking time for microwave cooking. It is best to watch what you are cooking closely to monitor its progress.

standing time
Many foods continue to cook when you take them out of the oven or microwave. If a recipe states that the food needs to 'stand' after cooking, be sure not to overcook the dish.

can sizes
The can sizes available in your supermarket or grocery store may not be the same as specified in the recipe. Don't worry if there is a small variation in size—it's unlikely to make a difference to the end result.

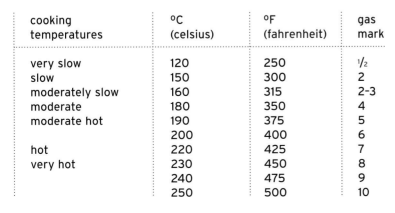

cooking temperatures	°C (celsius)	°F (fahrenheit)	gas mark
very slow	120	250	½
slow	150	300	2
moderately slow	160	315	2-3
moderate	180	350	4
moderate hot	190	375	5
	200	400	6
hot	220	425	7
very hot	230	450	8
	240	475	9
	250	500	10

index